The Pond

Written by Claire Llewellyn
Illustrated by Martin Sanders

Collins

We can see frogs.

We can see snails.

We can see dragonflies.

We can see pond-skaters.

We can see fish.

We can see a bird!

The Pond

frogs

dragonflies

fish

snails

a bird

pond-skaters

15

Ideas for guided reading

Learning objectives: Tracking the text in the right order, page by page, left to right, top to bottom, pointing while reading; reading on sight high frequency words; recognising printed words in a variety of settings, e.g. labels.

Curriculum links: Knowledge and Understanding of the World: Find out about features of living things; observe features of the natural world; find out about their environment

High frequency words: can, see, we, a

Interest words: pond, bird, frogs, fish, snails, dragonflies, pond-skaters

Word count: 34

Resources: whiteboard, pen

Getting started

- Read the title, and the names of the author and illustrator. Ask what the children can see on the front cover and read the blurb together.

- Walk through the book focusing on the illustrations. Discuss what the book is about (a nature trek by two children and their teacher) and what pond animals they find. Ask the children to point out the animal words.

- Discuss the pattern of text on each page ('We can see ...'). Model one-to-one matching, and ask the children to do the same.

Reading and responding

- Ask the children to read the book up to p13. During the reading, observe, prompt and praise each child in turn. Check for one-to-one matching, page turning and left-right directionality.

- Write we, can and see on your whiteboard and check if the children can read these words out of context.